# DISCOVER

# M A U I

## *The Valley Isle*

*Text by*

# STU DAWRS

*Photography by*

# RON DAHLQUIST

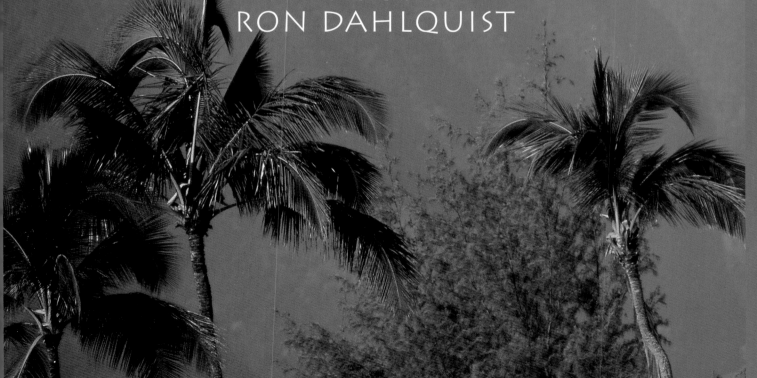

Clockwise from top left: *The ancient Hawaiian art of chanting. Winter surf crashes on the north shore. Stately Norfolk pines at sunset, upcountry. Francis Lono, Jr., of Hāna. Fishing nets adorn homes in Hāna. Palms silhouetted against the West Maui Mountains. Footprints in the sand. The old Hawaiian village of Kahakuloa.* Opposite, clockwise from top left: *Late afternoon clouds surround the peaks of the West Maui Mountains, seen from Lahaina. Jacob and Angel Mau share a special moment. Protea growing upcountry. Hula dancer at sunset, Kīhei. Experienced hands repair fishing net on Lānaʻi. Pebbles worn smooth with time. Keiki hula dancers Kiana Iwado and Rhame Mattos. The moon sets, a new day begins.* Ridges in ʻIao Valley.

CONTENTS

# E KOMO MAI

## WELCOME!

**K**UMULIPO, the 2,077-line Hawaiian chant that recounts the creation of the universe and all things in it, sings of the demigod Maui—a half-human trickster whose exploits are known and revered throughout Polynesia. It is said that Maui and his brothers brought the islands of Polynesia into existence by fishing them up from the ocean floor in one heroic tug. Part Prometheus, part Paul Bunyan, it was the prankster Maui who lassoed the sun, forcing it to move more slowly across the sky; Maui who stole fire from a crafty mud hen and gifted it to human-kind (nearly setting the world on fire in the process); and Maui who ultimately died at the powerful hands of the goddess Hina.

Fitting then that the only island in Polynesia to bear the name of a god should be the island of Maui—such is its power, beauty and magic. From the lunar desert of east Maui's Haleakalā Crater (the largest dormant volcano in the world) to the lush rainforests and bogs of the West Maui Mountains; from the verdant pasture lands of upcountry Maui on Haleakalā's western flank to the sugar white beaches and upscale resorts of Kapalua and Kāʻanapali—there are few places in the Pacific that can match Maui's grace and diversity.

Maui's recent history is as much the stuff of legend as the island's storied namesake was. In 1790, west Maui's Olowalu Beach became the infamous sight of what Hawaiians would come to refer to as "the day of spilled brains," when American sea-captain Simon Metcalfe—enraged over the theft of a small boat and the murder of one of his crew—ordered his men to open fire on a group of islanders whom he had invited out to his vessel. More than 100 people were murdered. Later, in an unrelated incident, Metcalfe managed to insult Kame-iamoku, a chief on the island of Hawaiʻi's Kona coast, who in turn vowed to destroy the next foreign sailors he saw—which turned out to be Metcalfe's son and his five-man crew, sailing the *Fair American* into the same Kona harbor a few days later.

Only the ship's mate, Isaac Davis, was spared as an acknowledgment of his bravery in battle. Later that same year another Hawaiʻi chief, Kamehameha I (soon to be known as Kamehameha the Great) embarked with Davis aboard the *Fair American* for Hāna, using the east Maui village (and the ship's cannons) as the starting point for a bloody campaign that would eventually unite all of the Hawaiian Islands under one ruler. Ultimately, west Maui's port of Lahaina would become Kamehameha's royal seat.

By the mid-1800s, Lahaina harbor was the central port of the American whaling fleet; today, it is part of the Humpback Whale National Marine Sanctuary and a prime winter destination for visitors hoping to catch a glimpse of one of these endangered giants.

For more than 100 years, sugar cane was king on Maui (as it was throughout the islands); today, with

Preceding pages: *2,250 foot ʻĪao Needle looms above the valley floor in ʻĪao Valley State Park.*
Above: *Petroglyph at Kukui Point, near Shipwreck Beach, Lānaʻi.* Background: *The steep canyon walls of ʻĪao Valley.* Opposite top: *Ālau Island as seen from Koki Beach, Hāna.*
Opposite bottom: *Busy Front Street in Lahaina at night.*

Opposite, top to bottom: *Aerial view of Kapalua. Cane fields viewed through wild bougainvillea in Spreckelsville on Maui's north shore. The resort area of Wailea, looking toward Kīhei and West Maui.*

Right: *Molokini crater, with Haleakalā in the background.* Bottom right: *Snorkelers enjoy the crystal clear waters and beautiful coral reef off Molokini.* Below: *Lei Day celebration at the Makawao Montessori School.*

the crop being produced far cheaper abroad, sugar has given way to diversified agriculture and tourism as Maui's chief money makers.

Things change and things remain the same. Like all of Hawai'i, the Aloha spirit is alive in Maui's residents, linking the upcountry farmer in Kula growing onions that are renowned as the sweetest in the world to the artist hawking his wares on a Saturday afternoon in Lahaina, shaded by one of the world's largest banyan trees. This is the true source of Maui's magic.

Today, visitors to the island can choose between stays in five-star west Maui resorts or visits to east Maui's Hāna (often called "the most Hawaiian spot" in the island chain) or even to Kahakuloa—the nearly inaccessible north Maui fishing village said to be a favorite destination of the demigod himself. The island's nearshore waters are home to some of the best surfing and windsurfing in the world. The tiny, crescent-shaped Molokini island, a three-mile boat ride from Maui's southwest shore, is a popular day-sailing destination and both Moloka'i and Lāna'i are short plane hops away. Adventurous hikers can spend the night in one of three cabins in the Haleakalā National Park. The less adventurous can spend an evening taking in the nightlife sights of Lahaina. Truly, Maui is a land of many faces.

*E komo mai:* Welcome to Maui.

Opposite top and bottom:
*The remote and rugged
coast at the ancient Hawaiian
village of Kahakuloa on Maui's
north shore.* Right: *Francis
Lono, Jr., caretaker of the
ancient Piʻilani Heiau.*
Below: *Kahakuloa village.*

# HĀNAU

## BIRTH

THE VOLCANIC CONES that form the Hawaiian islands are said to be the most massive natural structures on earth. After the island of Hawai'i, Maui is the second youngest island in the Hawaiian chain, and is located near the southeastern end of the Hawaiian archipelago—a volcanic necklace of some 130 islands, islets and shoals that stretches 1,600 miles across the North Pacific.

Every island in the Hawaiian chain was created by a single "hot spot" in the earth's mantle. It is estimated that, for as long as 100 million years, the plate of the earth's crust that lies beneath the Pacific Ocean has been inching northwest over this superheated vent. The mantle itself has remained stationary, thereby creating a string of islands that stretches from the oldest formations (the submerged Emperor Seamounts at the northwest end of the Hawaiian chain) to the site of the hot spot's current activity—the island of Hawai'i, at the southeastern end of the chain.

Thus formed by the same volcanic activity that created the entire Hawaiian chain, the island of Maui was once, during the glacial period, roughly twice its present size. Maui Nui, as this ancient island is sometimes referred to, was estimated to be 3,230 square miles—about three-quarters the current land mass of the island of Hawai'i. As the polar caps melted and sea levels rose, the low-points on this large island were submerged, forming the separate islands of Maui, Lāna'i, Moloka'i, Kaho'olawe and Molokini.

The Maui of today is the creation of two separate volcanoes—the 10,023-foot tall Haleakalā, which makes up all of east Maui, and the much older West Maui Mountains (the highest point being Pu'u Kukui, at 5,788 feet). The two volcanoes are bridged by an isthmus, created when lava flowing down Haleakalā's eastern flank joined with past eruptions from the West Maui Mountains. Both volcanoes are known as "shields"—so named because their shape resembles a medieval warrior's shield, as opposed to the more famous "composite cone" structure of volcanoes like Japan's Fuji and Washington State's St. Helens.

Though Pu'u Kukui (the name translates literally as "candlenut hill") is today dwarfed by the mass of Haleakalā, at one time the area was a single shield, with a crater measuring approximately five miles across. Eruptions, collapses and stream erosion have reshaped the entire mountain range, creating a series of spectacular cliffs and canyons that have led Maui to be rightfully nicknamed "The Valley Isle." The famed

*Above and background: Molten lava erupting and pouring into the sea from a vent in*
*Kilauea's east rift zone, on the Big Island of Hawai'i.*
*Opposite top: Afternoon mists and the sun's rays fill Waikapū Valley.*
*Opposite bottom: Cinder cone in Haleakalā Crater.*

*The island of Lāna'i was once a part of the land mass that included Maui, Lāna'i, and Kaho'olawe.*

Opposite, clockwise from top left: Afternoon colors fill the crater of Haleakalā. 'Īao Needle.

*Sunset at the Ulupalakua Ranch. The West Maui Mountains near Waiehu.*

'Īao Needle, rising like a finger 2,250 feet above sea level, is actually a remnant of the original Pu'u Kukui caldera, and a product of this natural erosion.

Estimated to be nearly one million years old, Haleakalā is far younger than its West Maui counterpart —which accounts for its much gentler slopes and intact, 7-mile long crater. With a land mass four times that of West Maui, the dormant volcano — which last erupted in the late 1700s — makes up the bulk of the island.

It has been pointed out that, when flying over Maui today, the outline of the island looks much like the torso of a man—or perhaps a demigod?—gazing down at the island of Kaho'olawe. West Maui in this sense is the island's head, with the fishing village of Kahakuloa at the back of the head, the stretch of beaches between Kapalua and Kā'anapali as the forehead, Olowalu as the nose and Mā'alaea as the base of the chin. The neck— that is, the isthmus— is bounded on the north by Kahu- lui and on the south by Kīhei. The body, with Hāna at the easternmost "waist," is made up entirely by the bulk of Haleakalā. For all of Haleakalā's impressive volume and West Maui's craggy valley terrain, at its widest points Maui is a mere 25 miles across from north to south and 40 miles from east to west.

Thus an island was born and has matured.

# GREAT MAUI

## KAHO'OLAWE, MOLOKA'I, LĀNA'I

WHILE THE LAND BRIDGES linking Maui, Moloka'i, Lāna'i and Kaho'olawe were submerged by rising sea levels millennia ago, the islands continue to be linked in a much more mundane fashion. What was once Maui Nui is now Maui County. Of Maui's three neighbors, only two—Moloka'i and Lāna'i—are populated. The third, Kaho'olawe, is presently uninhabitable. Though each island is a short hop from Maui, each has a distinct geography and history that belie any common past.

An admission: to say that Maui is the only island in Polynesia named after a god is a misstatement. Better to say that it is the only island currently named after a god. Kaho'olawe was originally known as Kanaloa, after one of the four major Hawaiian deities and a divinity much revered by *kāhuna 'anā'anā*—that is, sorcerers who practiced black magic. Created, according to Hawaiian cosmology, by the union of Wākea the Sky Father and Haumea-papa the Earth Mother, Kaho'olawe became the center of a disagreement between two goddesses, and is said to have been cursed into desolation—a curse that has been lived out time and again over the centuries.

In the early 1800s, Queen Ka'ahumanu banished criminals to the island; by the 1860s, goats and sheep were running slipshod over the native vegetation. In 1910, the Territory of Hawai'i named the entire island a forest reserve, but little was done to protect it—with one exception. In 1917, rancher Angus McPhee attempted to initiate a reforestation effort, planting thousands of native trees and eucalyptus windbreaks and—in one year—removing and selling some 13,000 goats.

A good start, but a failed effort ultimately. At the advent of World War II, the U.S. Navy took possession of Kaho'olawe, and through 1990 used the island as a bombing target, severely altering the landscape and leaving a legacy that will be years in the undoing.

In recent years, however, Kaho'olawe has shown signs of coming out from under its curse. In the late 1970s, the island served as a rallying point for a growing sense of Hawaiian pride. At the same time that Hawaiian cultural practices were experiencing a renaissance in the form of hula, music, language and traditional sports like outrigger canoeing, the Protect Kaho'olawe 'Ohana (PKO) was formed.

Above: *Moa'ula Falls, Hālawa Valley, Moloka'i*. Background: *The north coast of Moloka'i*.
Opposite top: *The Garden of the Gods on Lāna'i, with the island of Moloka'i in the distance*.
Opposite bottom: *The island of Kaho'olawe*.

An upcountry view of late afternoon sun setting over Kahoʻolawe and Molokini. Right: A couple enjoying the solitude on otherwise deserted Make Horse Beach, Molokaʻi.

Eventually this grass-roots organization would become the most visible face of a surging native Hawaiian activism. In the end, after nearly two decades of protest—including dangerous, covert landings on the island—Kahoʻolawe was finally returned to the people in 1990. Recently, cleanup efforts spearheaded by the PKO have begun anew.

The island of Molokaʻi stands in grand contrast to Kahoʻolawe's fate. With the exception of Niʻihau—a privately owned island where traditional Hawaiian ways are still adhered to and access by outsiders is strictly limited—Molokaʻi is literally the most Hawaiian of all the islands. It is the only other island in the Hawaiian chain where people of Hawaiian ancestry make up the majority of the population.

Once an island of refuge for defeated warriors and those who had broken the laws of the *kapu* system, like all Polynesian places of refuge, Molokaʻi was protected not by brute strength but by the chants of *kāhuna* and by the land's own *mana*—that is, its life force. Today, that power is manifested not only in an island that has managed to remain relatively rural, but in a people who are fiercely committed to preserving a vanishing way of life. Though the lights of Oʻahu are brightly visible from the western shores of the island and there is much pressure from developers hoping to heighten Molokaʻi's appeal to visitors, there are currently no traffic lights here; no fast food restaurants and no movie theaters. One has to wonder what could be more appealing.

*An aerial view of Honolua
Bay with the island of
Moloka'i in the distance.
Pages 20–21: The cliffs along
the northern coast of Moloka'i
are among the world's highest.*

What Moloka'i does have is a storied past and an unparalleled natural beauty. North Moloka'i's Kalaupapa, a peninsula bounded on one side by the ocean and on the other by a 1,500-foot *pali* (cliff), was the site of a leper colony where those suffering from the disease were exiled to die. This was where Joseph De Veuster, otherwise known as Father Damien, landed in 1873 on his selfless mission to bring hope to the colony. Today, Kalaupapa's residents—all former patients—live on the peninsula of their own free will, leading an occasional tour for visitors willing to brave the walk or donkey ride from above.

To the east of Kalaupapa the *pali* rises even higher, topping 1,750 feet at Kahiwa Falls—the spot that marks the world's tallest sea cliffs. Directly south, on the other side of the island, lies Kaunakakai—at three

blocks long, the island's main town. Driving highway 450 east from Kaunakakai provides a magnificent view into old Hawai'i, as ancient fishponds, *heiau* (temples) and more recent churches drift slowly past. The road eventually leads to Hālawa Valley, once the site of a small but thriving community that moved on after a 1946 tsunami destroyed most of the homes and taro fields. Today, the area is for the most part uninhabited, and features easy hikes to waterfalls, ponds and a beach where the valley opens up to the ocean.

Lāna'i, too, is an island of many stories. Once a forsaken land said to be inhabited by flesh-eating spirits, the 140 square-mile island is said to have been cleared of the evil beings by Prince Kaululaau, who tricked the ghouls into leaving after he was exiled to the island. Today Lāna'i is best known as the "Pineapple Island"

Opposite left: *The cemetery at St. Philomena, Father Damien's church, at Kalawao, Moloka'i.* Opposite right: *Waterfalls abound along the precipitous northern coast of Moloka'i.* Right: *Beginning snorkelers enjoy the calm waters in this tide pool at Mānele Bay, Lāna'i.*

—an apt name considering the island was once home to the largest pineapple plantation in the world.

If you want to get to know the people of this island, it's not hard to do. Virtually all of the island's 3,000 permanent residents live in Lānaʻi City. At an elevation of 1,600 feet, the city offers a cool change to the hot, red-dirt fields below.

Lānaʻi is an island most suited for outdoor adventures. Not far from Lānaʻi City is the Munro Trail, leading up through stands of Norfolk pines (planted in the early 20th century by New Zealand naturalist George Munro) to Lānaʻihale—at 3,370 feet, the highest point on the island and a perfect vantage point to survey much of Lānaʻi's topography, as well as catch glimpses of five of the other islands in the Hawaiian chain. From this point, one can also look down into the dizzying depths of Maunalei Gulch, the site of the final battle for warriors unsuccessfully attempting to defend the island from the advance of Kamehameha I near the turn of the 19th century.

On the southeast corner of the island lie the abandoned fishing villages of Lopa, Naha and Keomuku, all still guarded by the curses of *kāhuna*—it's said that if you climb the coconut trees here without saying the proper prayers, you will not come back down.

Beachcombers will want to head out to the island's eastern shore, where Shipwreck Beach features the rusting carcass of a liberty ship and smaller pieces of others strewn across the sand, in mute testament to the island's feared past as an inhospitable port in bad weather. Snorkelers should head south to the idyllic calm of Hulopoʻe Bay, which offers some of the best glimpses of undisturbed sea life in all of Hawaiʻi.

Maui Nui can be translated as "Great Maui"—a phrase that holds true for each of the islands that once made up this large landmass. Each may now be separated by both ocean and history, and yet all are linked by a certain subtle heritage. All are members of a long-standing, close-knit family.

Opposite top: *A honeymoon couple stops along the Munro Trail to enjoy the view of Lānaʻi and neighboring Molokaʻi.*
Opposite bottom: *Kayakers at Puʻu Pehe Rock, Lānaʻi.*
Right: *A view of Puʻu Pehe Rock from Shark's Cove, Lānaʻi.*

# THE HOUSE OF THE SUN

## HALEAKALĀ AND UPCOUNTRY MAUI

AT CERTAIN TIMES OF YEAR, when viewing Haleakalā from Maui's isthmus towns of Kahului and Kīhei, or from further west in Wailuku and Māʻalaea, the sun seems to rise directly out of the volcano's crater. Literally translated as "the house of the sun," Haleakalā is, for Polynesians, the site of an epic battle between the demigod Maui and his adversary, the sun. For geologists, botanists and casual observers, it is simply a natural wonder.

While rising 10,023 feet above sea-level, only a third of Haleakalā is visible—the remainder lies beneath the surface of the ocean, giving the volcano a true elevation from the sea-floor of nearly 30,000 feet and making it the world's largest dormant volcano. At 13,784 and 13,680 feet above sea level respectively, Mauna Kea and Mauna Loa on the island of Hawaiʻi are taller—and younger—than Haleakalā. However, Mauna Kea is considered to be extinct, and Mauna Loa is an active volcano, having erupted for 22 days in 1984. Haleakalā, which is believed to have last erupted in 1790, falls in the category between these two—neither active nor extinct. Though an eruption at this point is doubtful, the mountain is nevertheless considered to be merely "sleeping."

Three thousand feet deep, 7.5 miles long, 2.5 miles wide and with a total circumference of 21 miles,

Haleakalā's crater is easily one of the most impressive spots on earth. Walking across the crater's desert-like floor, hikers will eventually cross paths with nine cinder cones, ranging in height from 600 to 1,000 feet. It's no wonder that the island's earliest inhabitants considered this to be a place of great power, regularly using the crater as an induction ground for fledgling *kāhuna.* Likewise, the island's current residents have placed a high value on the volcano. In 1961, much of Haleakalā was designated as a national park. Currently, the entire park has been set aside as a nature preserve, and is home to a variety of rare flora and fauna, including the *nēnē* (Hawaiian goose) and silversword—a member of the immense daisy family that has, over the centuries, evolved into a phantasm of a plant found nowhere else in the world.

The outer slopes of Haleakalā, which make up the entire eastern half of the island, present an infinite variety of climates and landscapes—some natural, others the result of various human enterprises. At one time virtually all of Haleakalā was blanketed by forest. Though many lush areas remain, regions like the mountain's southern flank—sometimes referred to by locals as "behind the mountain"—are among the most severely altered life zones in all of Hawaiʻi. Ironically

Above: *Dan Cohen venturing out on a precipice overlooking Haleakalā crater.*
Background: *Sunrise at Haleakalā.*
Opposite: *A guided horseback trip on Sliding Sands Trail in Haleakalā crater.*

beautiful in its desolation, this area was once home to a large, closed canopy dry-land forest that was virtually impenetrable in spots. Most of the area has now been denuded by more than a century of cattle ranching, its trees giving way almost entirely to invasive African grasses that were imported to sustain grazing. While the upper reaches of this area were once moderately wet and it has been estimated that as many as 8,000 Hawaiians at one time lived in the south flank area known as Kahikinui (which literally translates as "great Tahiti," and may have been one of the first areas settled in Hawai'i), the loss of trees has utterly altered the climate, creating an arid and unlivable environment.

*Nēnē geese (Hawai'i's state bird) in Haleakalā crater. Right: A view of the crater from the summit. Bottom right: The silver-sword, which grows to a height of about 7 feet, blooms once and then dies. Opposite: Packing in supplies on the Halemau'u trail, Haleakalā.*

In recent years, however, the area has also become the site of a unique experiment. A group of mostly Hawaiian settlers known as Ka 'Ohana O Kahikinui (the family of Kahikinui) is attempting to revitalize the land along the lines of a traditional *ahupua'a*—an ancient and well-conceived system of apportionment in which the land was divided into large segments that stretched from mountain to sea, thereby providing each community with every resource needed to sustain life on an island. If the modern day pioneers of Kahikinui succeed, the region could very well become a model of sustainability for other areas throughout the Hawaiian chain and the Pacific.

"Upcountry" Maui, the area that makes up Haleakalā's broad western flank between the small agricultural towns of Makawao and Olinda in the north and the 18,000-acre Ulupalakua Ranch to the south, fared

Opposite: *A cinder cone in Haleakalā.* Above: *The Visitors Center overlooks the crater.* Right: *Hikers arriving at Palikū cabin in the crater.* Below: *A rainbow shines brightly in the meadow surrounding the cabin.*

Clockwise from top left:
*An unusual sight: A snowcapped summit of Haleakalā crater, emerging above the bank of thick clouds. Rustic fences add to the character of upcountry Maui. The grounds and tasting room at the Tedeschi Vineyards. John Armstrong harvesting a load of proteas at his Olinda farm. Bottom right: Ulupalakua Ranch in the late afternoon.*

somewhat better than the mountain's southern flank. Lying in an area that ranges from 1,500 to 4,000 feet above sea level, the moderately cool year-round temperatures (in winter, it can get as cold as 40 degrees Fahrenheit) and well-drained volcanic soil make the area ideal for both farming and ranching.

After clearing the native *koa* forests, early Hawaiians grew a variety of vegetables in Kula, the midway point between Upcountry's north and south boundaries. They traded the vegetables for lowland staples such as salt, fish and a variety of *limu* (edible seaweed). In the 19th century, farmers switched to potatoes to feed the burgeoning population of whalers in Lahaina. Now, the area not only produces as much as 2 million pounds of sweet Maui onions each year, but also four-fifths of the cabbage consumed yearly throughout the islands and a variety of other food crops. In addition, Kula is known for its tropical flower farms, which ship a wide variety of exotic blossoms worldwide. Further south, Ulupalakua Ranch is home to the 20-acre Tedeschi Vineyards, Hawai'i's first and best known winery.

Clockwise from top left: *Hui Aloha church, Kaupō. Jacaranda in bloom at the Haleakalā Ranch and Dairy. Masa Uradomo with his Maui-grown cabbage. Textures of the valleys and ridges in Kaupō. A lone cow grazing on the slopes of Haleakalā. The quaint town of Makawao. A bouquet of proteas grown in upcountry Maui. Pages 34–35: Cattle graze on the fertile slopes of Haleakalā.*

# NĀ HOʻOKELE
## THE NAVIGATORS

ALTHOUGH NO ONE knows exactly when the first Polynesian navigators landed on Hawaiʻi's shores, most date the intentional settlement by islanders from the south as taking place between 500 and 800 A.D. The islands were no doubt originally stumbled upon, but the incredible fact remains that the earliest navigators were able to find their way back and forth without instruments, using only the position of sun, moon and stars, cloud formations, the movements of fish, ocean currents and swell directions as guides to their destination. Having found these islands but no doubt ill-provisioned to settle them, the first of these navigators eventually returned home with tales of an uninhabited land of plenty to the north—tales that were preserved through ancient navigational chants in islands as far flung as Bora Bora, Moorea and Tahiti.

Numerous chants, stories and legends tell of repeated voyages between Hawaiʻi and Tahiti. Indeed, the name of the ocean channel that separates Maui, Kahoʻolawe and Lānaʻi suggests a strong link between the two island nations—Kealaikahiki translates literally as "the path to Tahiti." It is not hard to imagine Kealaikahiki pointing the way south to Tahiti for ancient mariners, just as it is reasonable to believe that massive Haleakalā would serve as a navigational point for north-bound sailors.

To understand the navigational prowess of Polynesia's ancient mariners, it helps to know the amount of ocean they were covering. The Hawaiian island chain is located at the extreme northern point of the Polynesian triangle, an area that is bounded on each side by legs extending more than 5,000 miles —southwest to New Zealand and southeast to Easter Island. (As further proof of the common roots of islanders throughout Polynesia, the language spoken on islands flung across the triangle is remarkably similar. For example, the word for an indigenous islander is *maori* in New Zealand, *maohi* in Tahiti and *maoli* in Hawaiʻi.)

It is generally agreed that Hawaiʻi was settled in two waves. The first planned migrations were from the islands that Spanish explorers called the Marquesas—11 southern hemisphere islands on the extreme eastern edge of Polynesia, roughly midway between Hawaiʻi and Easter Island. Traveling in double-hulled canoes that ranged in length from 60 to 80 feet and could comfortably carry up to 30 family members, these once fierce warriors continued to arrive for some 500 years, settling peacefully (there was no longer competition

*Above: A weathered outrigger canoe, Moʻorea, French Polynesia. Background: An aerial view of the beautiful lagoon at Bora Bora. Opposite top: Big Beach, Mākena, East Maui. Opposite bottom: Paddlers off Sugar Beach, Kīhei, Maui.*

Opposite: *Paddlers at sunset.*
Top: *An aerial view of southwest Maui's La Pérouse Bay and Āhihi-Kinau Natural Reserve.*
Above: *Mt. Otemanu rises from the sea on the island of Bora Bora.*

for land) and abandoning such habits as eating the bodies of their defeated foes.

The second wave of settlers came from the center of the Polynesian triangle—from Tahiti—during the 12th century. The dominant Tahitians quickly subjugated the original settlers, introducing new gods and a rigid set of laws known as the *kapu* system. Travel between Tahiti and Hawai'i is believed to have continued for an estimated 100 years, before abruptly—and without explanation—ceasing.

At this point, Hawai'i for the most part disappeared from Polynesian consciousness, remaining isolated for nearly 500 years until Captain James Cook set foot on the island of Kaua'i in 1778—assuring that Hawai'i would never again be truly secluded, and opening the door for an ongoing wave of white settlers that would change the island nation forever.

# THE ROAD LESS TRAVELED

## THE HĀNA HIGHWAY

"THE JOY OF TRAVELING," it's been said, "is not the destination but the journey." When it comes to the journey to Hāna, however, the reply to this adage would have to be "well, sort of." Here, the end and the means are equally rewarding.

The Hāna Highway (otherwise known as Route 36) begins quietly enough on the northern side of the isthmus that divides east and west Maui, just past Kahului airport in the sleepy town of Pā'ia. But things weren't always so idyllic here. At the turn of the 20th century, Pā'ia (which is alternately translated as "temporarily deaf" or "noisy") was the main portal into east Maui's sugar plantations, with a railroad line and a large, multi-ethnic population of field workers who lived in segregated housing known throughout Hawai'i as the "camps." During the town's heyday, in the 1930s, Pā'ia's population of 10,000 was the largest on the island.

Today, the town bustles with a different type of movement. After a decades-long slumber, Pā'ia re-awoke in the '70s, when hippies looking to "get away from it all" established themselves in the town and began to refurbish. The '80s saw a different kind of seeker, as windsurfing became a boom industry on Maui, centering around the now-famous beach of

Ho'okipa—considered to be one of the prime board-sailing locations in the world and a scant 10 minutes outside of town. Pā'ia itself mirrors these two influxes, with brightly colored storefronts, boutiques and restaurants that are, for the most part, geared toward tourists —be it traveling sailor or motorist on the road to Hāna.

It isn't until Route 36 turns into Route 360, about three miles outside of Pā'ia, that the more legendary aspects of the Hāna Highway come in to play. Carved out of the coastline in 1927 using only picks and shovels, the road rises up from sea level and through the small agricultural town of Ha'ikū. The vista begins to open up—and speeds begin to drop. In the 52 miles between Pā'ia and Hāna, there are some 600 turns and more than 50 one-lane bridges. Rounding any given hairpin corner, motorists are alternately greeted by sheer drops to the ocean, sometimes hundreds of feet below, and cascading waterfalls dropping through the backs of steep valleys.

Because the highway runs on the windward side of the island where rainfall is heaviest, the runoff has not only carved deep crags in the face of Haleakalā, but given rise to some unique modern folklore. Some old-timers recount tales of motorists who, trapped on

*Above: The famous road to Hāna, with its seemingly endless curves and narrow bridges.*
*The winding road almost forces visitors to slow down and enjoy the spectacular views.*
*Background: Lush tropical growth and one of the many streams along the road.*
*Opposite: Sunrise at Ālau Island, Hāna.*

Colorful shops line the streets in
the old plantation town of Pāʻia.
Once the main gateway to East
Maui's sugar plantations, the
town now serves as a jumping-off
spot for windsurfers headed to the
world famous beach at Hoʻokipa.

Left: *Windsurfers skimming across the water at Hoʻokipa.*
Bottom left: *A surfer at Pavillions (Hoʻokipa Beach Park).*
Below: *Windsurfers line the beach at Kanahā Beach Park.*
Opposite: *Windsurfers prepare to enter the surf at Hoʻokipa.*

*A view of the road to Hāna*
*as it follows the contours of*
*the northern coast of Maui.*
*Opposite: Lush Wailua Falls.*
*Pages 48–49: Getting a closer*
*look at Wailua Falls, near Hāna.*

opposite sides of a mudslide, would exchange cars and continue on their way!

As the road progresses, low-lying pasture lands and pineapple fields eventually give way to lush tropical rainforests. The effect, ultimately, is the feeling that one has somehow landed in a postcard.

Like much of Hawai'i, the trek to Hāna is full of a beauty that is both real and symbolic. Each bridge on this route has been given a name that, taken in total, is a poetic account of the experience of driving the Hāna Highway. From bridge number one (O'opuola— "life maturing") to 25 (Kūhiwa—alternately "precious love" or a special taboo) to 54 ('Ohe'o—"enduring pride"), the road is representative of a journey that is as much spiritual as it is physical—and the process of getting there is the perfect preparation for arrival in a town that is, in both geography and attitude, the exact opposite of west Maui's large-scale resorts.

# HEAVENLY HĀNA
## THE MOST HAWAIIAN SPOT

UNLIKE WEST MAUI'S bustling resorts, Hāna is most famous for what it doesn't have—namely, people. Said to be a favorite haunt of the demigod Maui, the history of this still sparsely populated area itself reads much like a legend.

Before the Hawaiian islands were united under Kamehameha I in 1796, Hāna was the location of a series of battles, most notably between Maui's chief Kahekili and Hawai'i's Kalaniōpu'u. Ka'uiki Hill, a red cinder promontory overlooking Hāna Bay, was the site of a standoff between the two—resulting ultimately in Kalaniōpu'u's surrender. Kamehameha I later launched his campaign to unite the islands from this same beachhead, eventually wresting Maui from Kahekili's son Kalanikupule after a bloody battle in west Maui's 'Īao Valley. Ka'ahumanu, Kamehameha's favorite wife and the woman considered most responsible for ending Hawai'i's strict set of laws known as the *kapu* system, was born in a cave near Hāna.

In 1849, Hawai'i's sugar industry was unwittingly founded in Hāna by a whaler named George Wilfong, when he disembarked four blubber pots and set them on a hill amid his small field of sugar cane. After crushing the cane and boiling the juice in the pots, Wilfong

was left with a high-grade sugar that he sold in the whaling port of Lahaina. From this inauspicious start was born King Sugar—an industry first nurtured by the California gold rush and later by the American Civil War, when the bulk of the sugar consumed on the continent was being produced by small Confederate farms that were, for the most part, destroyed in the latter stages of the conflict.

By the late 1880s, Hawai'i was the chief source of sugar for the United States, and the resultant shortage of laborers led to an immigrant boom from Japan, China, Portugal, the Philippines and Puerto Rico; cane bosses would arrive from Scotland, Germany and the United States. Along with the area's original inhabitants, all would eventually become a part of Hāna's present day population. And though Wilfong could hardly have foreseen it, the industry that he spawned would eventually lead to a low point in Hawaiian history. On January 17, 1893, on the island of O'ahu, Queen Lili'uokalani and the Hawaiian monarchy were forcibly overthrown by a small group of U.S.-backed growers and merchants who sought an easing of U.S. import tariffs and stronger ties to the continent.

Full of stories, Hāna nonetheless remains a quiet

Above: *Fishing boats in Hāna Bay.* Background: *'Ohe'o Gulch, Kīpahulu.*
Opposite top: *The rugged Hāna coastline.* Opposite bottom: *The peaceful village of Hāna as seen from Hāna Bay.*

Left: An aerial view of Hāna
Bay and town. Above: One
of several waterfalls along the
road to Kīpahulu. Below:
Waiʻanapanapa State Park is
known for its black sand beach
and lava rock formations.

*Lovely contrasts of the*
*Wai'anapanapa coastline.*
Right: *Ka'uiki Head*
*lighthouse, Hāna Bay.*

town, with a population of little more than 2,000. Sugar has long since been replaced by ranching and flower farming. Those unfamiliar with the area might drive past without even slowing down—but that would be their loss. Visitors willing to take the time are always rewarded. How often is it that one can visit the birthplace of a queen? Or a site that fits so prominently in both legend and history?

Those interested in easy hikes can follow the trail to Ka'uiki Hill—which tradition says was a lover of Maui's daughter before the demigod turned him into the promontory. Once there, the panoramic view makes one understand why this spot was used until very recently by fishermen as a site for spotting schools swimming in the bay below. And of course, there are the people of Hāna—living away from the hustle of Hawai'i's urban centers, these residents have helped preserve the true spirit of aloha, a treasure that is worth the journey in itself.

# MAUI'S STRIFES
## FIRE · LAND · THE SUN

PERHAPS IT IS because Maui was half-human, but there are certain elements of the divine, the comic and even the profane in his actions—often depending on who is telling the story. In Tonga, for example, the narratives have much to do with the slaying of monsters; in the Marquesas, the stories have a distinctly erotic flair; and in the Society Islands, Maui loses his prankster aspects altogether to become an up-standing member of society, one who snares the sun to give his brother, Maui-mua, more time to build his temples.

In Hawai'i, Maui's character is best seen in three of his more famous exploits (referred to as *kaua* or "strifes" in the Kumulipo)— the theft of fire as a gift for humans, the 'fishing up' of the islands, and the snaring of the sun.

### FIRE

The Kumulipo tells us that Maui's first feat was to steal fire from the sacred 'alae—the Hawaiian mud hen. Though the goddess Hina of the Fire had already gifted Maui with fire by giving him her flaming fingernails, the demigod was somewhat clumsy with them, eventually dropping each one (with, one can imagine, near disastrous results). Having lost Hina's gift, Maui went hunting for the crafty mud hens, finally finding them in Wai'anae (on the west coast of the island of O'ahu) where they were roasting bananas. However, every time Maui approached, the 'alae would scratch out the fire before he could reach it.

At long last, he managed to capture the smallest of the mud hens, and threatened to wring its neck if it did not tell him where to find fire. First the bird told him that fire was in the stalk of the taro plant; then in the stalk of the ti leaf. Maui tried in vain to draw fire from these plants, rubbing the leaves until the stalks were hollowed out— as they still are today. The 'alae finally acquiesced, showing Maui how to find fire in hau and sandalwood trees. (The Hawaiian word for sandalwood is 'iliahi, which, if broken into two words, literally translates as "a fiery surface.") In punishment for the mud hen's trickery, Maui rubbed a red streak into the bird's head, which all 'alae (ironically now an endangered species) have today.

### LAND

The story tells us that before Maui came along there was very little land for the people to live on. Wanting to help, Maui descended into the land of the dead and peti-

Above: *Luminous afternoon mists engulf 'Iao Needle and its surrounding ridges.*
Background: *The West Maui Mountains and ocean bathed in afternoon light.*
Opposite: *An almost preternatural cloud formation above Pā'ia. An ancient Hawaiian belief held that some gods could assume the form of clouds.*

tioned an ancestress to make him a fishing hook. She did, fashioning the legendary hook *Manai a ka lani* ("come here from the heavens") from her own jawbone.

Maui then captured another sacred *'alae*. Using the mud hen as bait, Maui passed the hook on to his sister Hina of the Sea, who plunged into the depths and placed the hook in the mouth of Pimoe (sometimes called "Old One Tooth"), who held all the land below the surface of the sea.

Maui then exhorted his brothers to paddle a canoe with all their strength, warning them not to look back. For two days they paddled, fighting Pimoe. Unfortunately, just when it appeared that they had won the battle and Pimoe was surfacing, one of the brothers looked over his shoulder—and so, instead of one large land mass, humans were left with groups of islands scattered throughout Polynesia.

## THE SUN

Maui's most famous exploit involves his capture of the sun. In older times, people could not get enough to eat because there were not enough daylight hours to fish or farm. Maui's own mother could not dry her *tapa* (bark) cloth because the sun raced too quickly across the sky.

Maui went to his blind grandmother, who lived on the slopes of Haleakalā and was responsible for cooking the sun's bananas, which he ate every day as he passed. Maui's grandmother advised him to weave a number of strong ropes, each with a noose on the end (variations of the story say that the ropes were made either from coconut fiber or his sister's hair).

One morning, as the sun began to rise out of Haleakalā, Maui positioned himself—snaring each of the sun's 16 rays as they peeked over the crater's rim. The sun, now trapped and defenseless, had to bargain for his life. So it was that Maui forced the sun to move more slowly across the sky and Haleakalā became its permanent home.

*Silversword in full bloom, Haleakalā.*

# MERCILESS SUN

## LAHAINA

OVER THE LAST 170 YEARS, Lahaina has seen its share of change. Once an exclusive surfing ground for Hawaiian royalty, the strategically placed town was established as Kamehameha I's royal seat after he consolidated his power over all of the islands in the 1790s. Between 1820 and 1870, the easy berthing offered by Lahaina harbor made it the prime Pacific anchorage for America's whaling fleet— and a boisterous stomping ground for sailors setting foot on land for the first time in months. At commercial whaling's peak, according to an 1846 census, Lahaina counted 429 whaling ships, 882 grass houses, 115 adobe huts, 59 wood or stone homes and a whopping 3,557 residents. Hawai'i's first western structure, the Brick Palace, was built here by Kamehameha I in 1801.

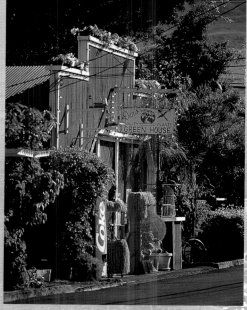

Lahaina was also one of the first landfalls for missionaries in Hawai'i, who arrived at this Maui port in 1823—and who would eventually change so much of Hawaiian life. Needless to say, the interactions between the whalers (who had first arrived in 1819 aboard the *Balena* from Massachusetts) and the missionaries were far from cordial. The drunken sailors regularly clashed with the Congregationalists. Legend even has it that more than one cannonball was launched from the harbor into the vicinity of a certain Reverend Richards'

Lahaina home—perhaps without the exact intention of sending him to meet his maker, but surely with the hope of putting the fear of God into him.

In the end, where curfews and prayer failed, time eventually won out. By the late 1860s, the whaling industry was all but dead, and Lahaina returned to a quieter, slightly more starched way of life. In the meantime, the missionaries were impacting life in other ways. The first school to be built west of the Rockies, Lahaina-luna ("above Lahaina") was erected here by Congregationalist missionaries in 1831; Hawai'i's first newspaper was printed here in 1834.

And of course, there was sugar. The Pioneer Sugar Mill was established in the 1860s, and for a number of years after the decline of the whaling industry, it was the chief source of income for the once booming town.

A century after the mill was founded, a second industry took root on Maui's western shores. In 1962, foreseeing the impact that tourism would eventually have on the island, developers began cleaning up a section of beach just to the west of Lahaina, which Pioneer Sugar Mill had for years been using as a dumping ground. This trash heap would eventually become Kā'anapali, one of the world's premiere resort areas and

*Above: Dan's Greenhouse in Lahaina specializes in exotic birds and plants.*
*Background and opposite: Lahaina harbor seen from the air.*

Above: *Late afternoon light on the West Maui Mountains and cane fields.* Right: *The old Pioneer Mill, Lahaina.* Below: *The Sugar Cane Train travels from Lahaina to Kā'anapali.* Opposite top and bottom: *Shops abound on Front Street in Lahaina.*

an economic boon for Lahaina. The Lahaina, Kā'anapali and Pacific Railroad, which used to chug its way down from the mill to Kā'anapali beach to deliver cane to waiting barges, today carries on with a completely different cargo. Now known as the Sugar Cane Train, the line is a popular day-ride for families.

Even though Lahaina proper stretches for some four miles along the sun-baked west Maui coast (*la haina* translates literally as "merciless sun"), most visitors find that the bulk of the town's modern-day attractions are to be found in the mile-long stretch of central Lahaina that is cut through by Front Street. Along this road and on its branching tributaries lies a network of shops, boutiques and restaurants that provide a full day's wandering.

Lahaina's famed banyan tree, planted in 1873 to honor the golden anniversary of the Congregationalist missionaries, marks the eastern end of Front Street and

Opposite top: *The historic Baldwin Home Museum.*
Opposite bottom: *Wo Hing Temple, a Lahaina landmark.*
Above: *A rainbow arcs behind the* Carthaginian II, *a replica of a 19th-century whaling brig.*
Pages 66–67: *A sweeping panorama of the Pioneer Inn and Lahaina Harbor.*

is in itself a major attraction. Now one of the largest of its kind in the world, the banyan is a gathering place for artists selling their wares and anyone else looking for a shaded break from the blistering noon sun.

A westerly stroll down Front Street yields up other memorable sights including the Pioneer Inn, which was built in 1901 and has housed such distinguished guests as Errol Flynn and Spencer Tracy; Baldwin Home, which served as a dispensary from the 1830s through 1868 and features a Steinway piano built in 1859; and the remains of the Brick Palace, built in 1801. Anchored nearby is the *Carthaginian II,* a replica of a 19th-century whaling brig, that now serves as a floating museum for exploring whaling's past and celebrating the future of whales themselves.

Still further offshore is one of Lahaina's real treats. Beginning in November and peaking in February, the

famed North Pacific humpbacks make their annual migration to Hawai'i, with most gathering in waters off Maui and—to a lesser extent—Hawai'i's Kona coast.

During whale-watching season, when it seems that Maui's waters are full to capacity with the gentle giants and sightings are an everyday occurrence on the island's south and west shores, it's hard to believe that these 45-foot, 40-ton mammals have been overhunted to the brink of extinction. Sadly true—at the turn of

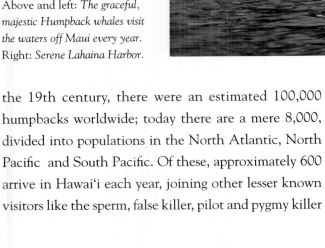

Above and left: *The graceful, majestic Humpback whales visit the waters off Maui every year.* Right: *Serene Lahaina Harbor.*

the 19th century, there were an estimated 100,000 humpbacks worldwide; today there are a mere 8,000, divided into populations in the North Atlantic, North Pacific and South Pacific. Of these, approximately 600 arrive in Hawai'i each year, joining other lesser known visitors like the sperm, false killer, pilot and pygmy killer

whales, all of which are found in the islands at various times. (It's interesting to note that although Hawaiians had a vast knowledge of the ocean and names for virtually every fish, all whales were referred to by one of two generic names—either *koholā* for whale or *palaoa* for sperm whale.)

Though hunters of both whales and salvation are now a part of Lahaina's storied past, the town continues to draw adventurous visitors from across the globe, enticing them with a palpable sense of history; of a past that has somehow managed to reach across nearly two centuries, informing every aspect of life under the merciless sun.

Top: *The Carthaginian II at sunset.* Above: *Rusted anchor chain.* Right: *Evening lights sparkle along Front Street.*

# 32 FLAVORS
## MAUI'S BEAUTIFUL BEACHES

IN THE NORTH there is Ho'okipa, considered by many to be the windsurfing capital of the world; facing south is Mā'alaea, known to surfers across the globe as the world's fastest wave; to the west is Kā'anapali's four-mile run of crystalline sand, attracting sun-worshipers from every corner of the Earth.

With 120 miles of coastline, Maui has more swimmable beaches than any other island in the Hawaiian chain and, it seems, no two are alike. Though locals tend to have one or two favorites, for visitors this can present a bit of a problem. Having to choose between more than 32 very good destinations is no easy task.

In terms of swimming and sun-bathing, the best beaches on the island are to be found on the 18-mile stretch along the west and southwest edge of west Maui, from Kapalua on the westernmost tip down to Olowalu.

With the exception of the winter months, when the surf can be dangerous, Kapalua is an ideal family beach. There is good swimming, snorkeling and (for the experienced) bodysurfing. Moving south, one next encounters the beaches of Kā'anapali—just as beautiful as Kapalua, but slightly harder to reach. Though state law requires that the public have access to all beaches, the beaches of Kā'anapali are bordered by hotels and there are occasionally problems finding parking. Of the beaches in this area, Black Rock provides the best snorkeling.

Further south, water lovers come across Lahaina Beach (which is convenient, but not particularly secluded); Launiupoko and Puamana (good views and grassy areas for lounging, but only mediocre swimming); Olowalu (good swimming); and Papalaua, (an ideal beach for those seeking seclusion with its tiny patches of sand fringed by thorny kiawe trees).

Traveling on, one comes first to Mā'alaea (which is really only a good stop for highly skilled surfers) and then to a series of increasingly secluded beaches in the Wailea area, all culminating in one of the gems of the island—Mākena. A favorite of both locals and visitors, Mākena is something of an "alternative" beach, offering enough seclusion to make it the preferred haunt for nude sunbathers and all others just looking to get away from it all.

On the eastern end of the island, like everything else to be found in Hāna, there are some superb beaches—the ethereal Red Sand Beach and the well protected Hāna Bay being particular standouts. Also not to be overlooked are the Seven Sacred Falls, a series of freshwater pools fed by light waterfalls that overlook a roiling ocean mere yards away.

Such decisions! Even in paradise, life can be rough.

Above: Kathleen Souki dances the traditional hula kahiko on the beach at Wailea.
Background: Big Beach, at Mākena State Park, one of Maui's favorite beaches.
Opposite: Mākena State Park and Big Beach.

Clockwise from top left: *From Keʻanae the beauty of the rugged north Maui coastline can be seen. A couple enjoys the solitude of the beach at Māʻalaea Bay. Tidepool discoveries at Keawakapu. A net fisherman at Ulua Beach. Cane fields and the West Maui Mountains near Olowalu. The famed resort area of Kāʻanapali. Kapalua Beach.*

Opposite, clockwise from top left: *Kayakers at Sharks Cove, Lānaʻi. Little Beach, Big Beach and Puʻuōlaʻi. Ulua Beach in Wailea. A pencil urchin at Keawakapu. Wailea Resort area. Wailea Beach. Honeymooners enjoy the Molokini view. A snorkeler at Āhihi-Kinau Natural Reserve. Pages 76-77: Ulua Beach.*

# MAUI NŌ KA O'I

STANDING ON THE WESTERN RIM of Haleakalā, looking east with the late afternoon sun at your back, a phenomenon called Specter of the Brocken sometimes occurs. With the setting sun's oranging light filtered through light clouds and onto the denser fog that has gathered in the crater below, a circular rainbow appears.

Suddenly, an apparition materializes in the center of the rainbow. Raise your hand to wave and the spirit responds; call out, and you may get an echo in reply. Of course, the specter is your own shadow, but the ephemeral quality of this experience—at once both human and heavenly—is a fitting summation of all that Maui is. There the shadow stands, as silent testament to what some, perhaps slightly numbed by daily encounters with this magic land, may have grown to take for granted: *Maui Nō Ka O'i*.

"Maui indeed is the best."

Above left: *Olena Horcajo with pretty tropical flowers.* Above center: *The Steve Macres family.*
Above right: *Lovely Kelly Chun.* Bottom: *Jacob and Angel Mau.* Background: *Hiking into
Palikū, Haleakalā.* Opposite top: *Late afternoon at Polo Beach, on the south shore.*
Opposite bottom: *The West Maui Mountains and 'Īao Valley from Spreckelsville.*
Page 80 top: *The colors of dusk from Launiupoko Park.* Page 80 bottom:
*A lone surfer checks out the waves at Kū'au on the north shore.*